ESSENTIAL TIPS

dog care

This book is our gift to you. It has been created to get you off to a great start, and ensure a long and happy life with your new puppy. Enclosed are all the essential tips you need to raise a healthy dog, including health signs and symptoms to look out for, plus the easiest ways you can protect your pet from parasite infestations and the illnesses that they can cause. Your team at VCA is here for you every step of the way for advice, care and support, so call or visit us any time.

AT VCA ANIMAL HOSPITALS, WE'VE GOT THEM COVERED

I protected him

Important safety information

Serious adverse reactions have been reported following concomitant extra-label use of ivermectin with spinosad alone, one of the components of ComboGuard chewable tablets. Treatment with fewer than three monthly doses after the last exposure to mosquitoes may not provide complete heartworm prevention. Prior to administration of ComboGuard, dogs should be tested for existing heartworm infection. Use with caution in breeding females. The safe use of ComboGuard in breeding males has not been

Penguin
Random
House

Produced for Dorling Kindersley by
Sands Publishing Solutions
4 Jenner Way, Eccles, Aylesford, Kent ME20 7SQ

Editorial Partners	David & Sylvia Tombesi-Walton
Design Partner	Simon Murrell
Project Editor	Chauney Dunford
Project Art Editor	Elaine Hewson
US Editor	Jill Hamilton
US Senior Editor	Shannon Beatty
Managing Editor	Penny Warren
Producer, Pre-production	Heather Blagden
Producer	Rebecca Parton
Art Director	Jane Bull
Publisher	Mary Ling
Special Sales Creative Project Manager	Alison Donovan
Written by	David & Sylvia Tombesi-Walton
Consultant	Kim Bryan

This edition published in 2018
First American edition 2015
Published in the United States by DK Publishing
1450 Broadway, Suite 801, New York, NY 10018

A catalog record for this book is available from the Library of Congress.
ISBN 978-1-4654-5389-1

DK books are available at special discounts when purchased in bulk for sales promotions,
premiums, fund-raising, or educational use. For details, contact: DK Publishing Special
Markets, 1450 Broadway, Suite 801, New York, NY 10018 or SpecialSales@dk.com.

Printed and bound in Canada

A WORLD OF IDEAS:
SEE ALL THERE IS TO KNOW

www.dk.com

101 ESSENTIAL TIPS

DECIDING ON A DOG

1 IS A DOG RIGHT FOR YOU?

Dogs are joyful animals that bring companionship and fun into any household, but we must take care of their needs. These include food, shelter, and veterinary care, but also affection and physical and mental stimulation. Do you have time for at least one daily walk, ideally two? Do you have a safe, enclosed yard in which the dog can run around?

Playtime is important for dogs

Dogs and children can become the best of friends

2 ARE YOU RIGHT FOR A DOG?

Before getting a dog, be aware that costs—food, vaccinations and other veterinary expenses, insurance, kennels when you go on vacation—will add up. Consider your lifestyle, too: do you have the time and space to give a dog a stress-free environment for its entire lifetime? Can you cope with a dog and young children? Are you ready to pick up after your dog in public places?

3 LEGAL RESPONSIBILITIES

In the US, you must license your dog annually and have proof of up-to-date rabies vaccination; put the numbered tag on the dog's collar. You must also keep your dog under proper control, on a leash if the situation dictates. There are laws regarding your duty to care for a dog, and protect it from pain, suffering, injury, and disease.

Small now, but what about later?

CHOOSING A PUPPY

4

Everyone loves a puppy! But unless that little ball of fluff with a squeaky bark is a Chihuahua or other small breed, it won't stay that size for long. Seeing your puppy's parents will indicate how big it will grow, especially with a purebred dog; if it's a mixed-breed, be prepared for anything. Puppies are especially good for very young children, since they can grow up together, forming a lifelong bond.

CHOOSING AN ADULT DOG

5

One advantage of adult dogs over puppies is that they have already developed their personalities, so you know what you are getting. An adult dog is also more likely to have been neutered, saving you the expense for this procedure. Puppies will need a lot of your time and attention initially, whereas most adult dogs are already housebroken, for example. On the other hand, adult dogs may have bad habits that need to be corrected.

Tilted head implies request

EXPRESS YOURSELF
An adult dog will probably have no qualms about telling you what it needs.

WHICH SEX?

6

There are some points to bear in mind when it comes to choosing a dog based on its gender. Unneutered young males can be problematic when their sex hormones are raging, while females go into heat twice a year, which means extra work for the owner, as well as dealing with advances from male dogs and, potentially, puppies.

BE WISE TO THE SIZE
Within the same breed, the male/female size difference may be a decisive factor.

7 CHOOSING A PUREBRED

The advantage of a purebred dog is that you will have a fair idea of its behavioral traits, since these are breed-specific. You will also be able to predict its adult size, how much exercise it will need, food requirements, and so on. Plus, you will receive certification of the dog's lineage, essential if you want to enter it into dog shows. On the down side, purebred dogs can be expensive to buy, and some breeds have inherent health problems.

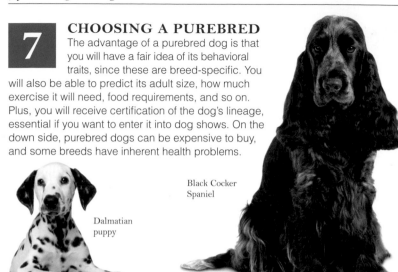

Black Cocker Spaniel

Dalmatian puppy

8 CHOOSING A MIXED-BREED DOG

Even if money is no object, you don't have to opt for a purebred pooch. Shelters are full of mixed-breed dogs (random, unknown crosses) looking for good, loving homes. One of the advantages of mixed breeds is that they do not tend to suffer from breed-related disorders. Furthermore, they often have big, fun-loving personalities.

SIZING UP THE SITUATION
It can be almost impossible to predict how large a mixed-breed dog will grow, due to its random—and perhaps unknown—parentage.

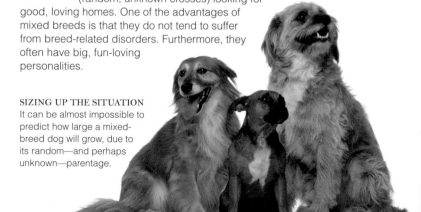

9 COATS TO CONSIDER

Some dogs shed more, and others require extra care—for example, dogs with long, silky coats need daily grooming to prevent matting, while poodles and some terrier breeds need clipping or stripping, as well as grooming. Grooming is a good chance to spend time handling your dog and checking it over for any health issues.

LONG
These coats need more care than other coat types. Long coats can mask issues such as injuries or weight problems, so be alert to these when grooming your dog.

SMOOTH
The easiest of all the coat types, smooth coats require little equipment other than a comb and a soft brush. They should not be bathed too often because this washes away their natural oils.

WIRY
These coats need a lot of combing or they will get matted. Clipping or stripping every 6–8 weeks is also an option.

CURLY
Every couple of months, these nonmolting coats need a clip and a bath. Excess hair in the ears should be plucked.

10 HOW MUCH SPACE DO YOU NEED?

The amount of space you need will depend both on the size and age of the dog you acquire and on the amount of exercise it receives. A mid-sized energetic dog that gets out a lot may be content simply to lounge around when indoors.

Chihuahua—tiny, but it may enjoy running around

SPRINGING INTO ACTION
Springer Spaniels require an enormous amount of exercise and space, so a small home is not for them.

11 CONSIDERING SMALL BREEDS

Even if you have decided that you want a small dog—maybe because you live in an apartment—there is still many breeds available to you. As you would expect, small dogs come in all shapes, colors, and temperaments, so there is plenty to consider when picking the right breed for you. Do not allow small dogs to get away with undesirable behavior (growling, food aggression) because of their size. You still need to be the leader of the pack.

Longhair is less common type of Chihuahua

CHIHUAHUA
This ever-popular toy breed can be wary of big dogs, but it is outgoing and low maintenance in exercise and grooming.

SHIH TZU
Friendly to humans and animals, this happy breed has a long, thick coat that needs to be groomed every day.

Hind legs are strong and muscular

Short, wide back

PUG
This small breed needs little exercise and grooming and has a pleasing— if independent— personality.

JACK RUSSELL
This fun family favorite is an active, energetic breed that needs mental stimulation as well as regular exercise.

Shorthair's glossy coat requires minimal grooming

OTHER SMALL BREEDS
There is a whole host of small breeds to choose from, and those illustrated here are just the tip of the iceberg. Others include: Border Terrier, Fox Terrier, Yorkshire Terrier, West Highland Terrier, Lhasa Apso, Pembroke Welsh Corgi, Pekingese, Bichon Frisé, Cavalier King Charles Spaniel, Papillon, as well as miniature versions of the Schnauzer and Poodle, and the Doberman-lookalike Miniature Pinscher.

DACHSHUND
These recognizable spirited dogs seem to be unaware of their diminutive size; their courage is beyond compare.

12 CONSIDERING MEDIUM-SIZE BREEDS

A medium-size breed is a great choice, size-wise, for the family home. These breeds make up the great majority of dogs that you will see on leashes in the streets and in recreational areas and hiking spots. Kids who are old enough to run around love playing tag and ball games with their similarly sized canine companions, and a real bond often develops between them as the pair grow up together.

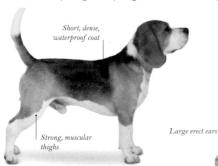

Short, dense, waterproof coat

Strong, muscular thighs

Long, silky ears tend to need regular washing

ENGLISH COCKER SPANIEL
This breed is a bundle of energy that needs lots of exercise. It is also quite high in grooming requirements.

BEAGLE
Friendly and anxious to play, Beagles make ideal family pets but need a lot of exercise, as well as a good degree of obedience training.

Large erect ears

Short, fine, smooth coat

FRENCH BULLDOG
Despite looking a little gruff, this muscular, energetic breed is affectionate and dependable.

Strong, straight forelegs

BORDER COLLIE
Faithful and obedient, this highly intelligent breed needs a great deal of regular exercise and mental stimulation.

OTHER MEDIUM-SIZE BREEDS
The list of medium-size dogs is a lengthy one. Some of the other popular breeds include: Whippet, English Springer Spaniel, Airedale Terrier, American Cocker Spaniel, Bull Terrier, Staffordshire Bull Terrier, Brittany, Standard Schnauzer, Shar-Pei, and Shetland Sheepdog.

13 CONSIDERING LARGE BREEDS

Big dogs are not necessarily the most energetic, although some certainly require a lot of exercise. What they all need, though, is enough living space, so these breeds are only suitable for those with large houses, ideally with a decent-sized yard, too. Large dogs, in particular, really benefit from obedience training.

AFGHAN HOUND
These intelligent, friendly dogs thrive on mental stimulation. They need a lot of care to keep their coat in good condition.

Deep, broad muzzle and square head

BOXER
Loyal and loving toward friends and family, this excitable breed needs obedience classes from a young age.

Wedge-shaped muzzle with black nose

Coat may be yellow, black, or chocolate

Broad, powerful thighs

LABRADOR
Great for families, this gentle giant enjoys playtime and needs fairly regular exercise.

GERMAN SHEPHERD
Frequent exercise is needed, but the breed is receptive to training and loyal to its master.

GREAT DANE
This breed needs a lot of exercise and space in the home. You may need a large income to cover its dietary requirements.

OTHER LARGE BREEDS

There are many more large breeds than shown on this page. Among the best known and most popular are: Newfoundland, St. Bernard, Rottweiler, Bullmastiff, Japanese Akita, Bloodhound, Doberman, Irish Wolfhound, Chow Chow, Standard Poodle, Dalmatian, Old English Sheepdog, Collie, Greyhound, Rhodesian Ridgeback, Hungarian Viszla, Irish Setter, German Pointer, Golden Retriever, and Weimaraner.

A FRIEND IN NEED
Adopting a dog from a rescue shelter is not only a very affordable option, it also gives you the chance to do a good deed.

14 RESCUE SHELTERS

If you are not adamant about having any particular breed or type of dog, try your local rescue shelter. In fact, they are well worth visiting even if you do have fixed ideas: it's surprising how many purebreds are abandoned. These animals—young, old, and everything in between—are desperately in need of a good home, especially the older ones, which are all too often overlooked in favor of cute puppies.

15 REPUTABLE BREEDERS

If you opt to acquire a dog from a breeder, it is important to go to a good one, and that means putting in many hours of research. Start by asking the owners of breeds you like where they got their dogs from. Go to dog shows, too, and ask around for recommendations; word of mouth is always a good way to find a reputable breeder. The breeder should be able to supply you with all the necessary health and pedigree documentation.

CLEAN AND HAPPY
A good breeder should keep the pups in a clean environment in which the animals are happy.

16 QUESTIONS TO ASK

Especially in the case of breeders, there are certain questions that should be addressed. Are the dogs taken out to a toilet area regularly? (If so, housebreaking will usually be simpler.) Are the pups well socialized? Ask if they are being raised indoors, but look around, too, for evidence that they are.

SEE THE PARENTS
You should be able to see a puppy's mother, and maybe even the father, at a purebred breeder. If the mother is not there, you cannot be sure the puppies were bred there or verify their upbringing. Many people see puppies before they are fully weaned to decide which one they want. While it is unlikely a rescue shelter will have a puppy's mother, it is worth asking, in case they came in together or she arrived pregnant.

YOUR NEW FRIEND

17 DOG-PROOF YOUR HOME

Before you bring your new dog to live with you, make sure that your home provides a safe environment for it. Dogs like to investigate everything, so invest in a few childproof latches to prevent them from exploring food and china cabinets, and buy garbage cans with securely closing lids. It may also be worth purchasing some safety covers for any electric outlets not in use.

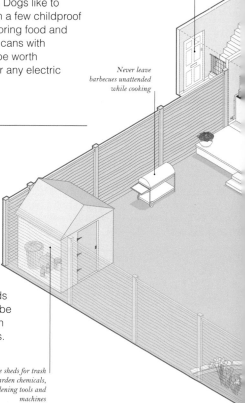

Keep front door closed to prevent "dash for freedom"

Never leave barbecues unattended while cooking

18 DANGERS IN THE HOME

Some substances routinely found in the home are toxic for dogs and could be potentially fatal if ingested. These include stone fruits, chocolate, cleaning products, human painkillers, antifreeze, and some house plants, such as cyclamen. Keep them out of reach. Long cords from curtains and blinds may also be hazardous for curious dogs, as can needles, thread, and rubber bands.

Use lockable sheds for trash cans, garden chemicals, and gardening tools and machines

19 DOG-PROOF YOUR YARD

Wait until your dog is familiar with and comfortable in its new home before allowing it to go outside. Use this time to dog-proof your yard. Make sure there are no holes or gaps in the fences that your dog would be able to get through; also make sure the height is sufficient to deter any jumping over, and that it cannot be dug under. Hedges are not viable yard perimeters for dogs. Fence gates should be kept closed, preferably sprung to shut automatically.

20 DANGERS IN THE YARD

The dangers in the yard are similar to those in the home—that is, toxic substances such as weedkillers, pesticides and slug and snail poisons, and wood preservatives. Store every container in a dog-proof shed, along with sharp and heavy gardening tools. Other hazards include toxic plants, such as foxgloves, mistletoe berries, and yew bark, needles, and seeds. If you have a puppy, fence off water features.

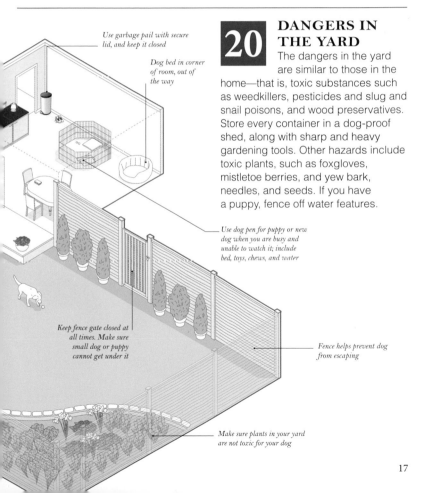

Use garbage pail with secure lid, and keep it closed

Dog bed in corner of room, out of the way

Use dog pen for puppy or new dog when you are busy and unable to watch it; include bed, toys, chews, and water

Keep fence gate closed at all times. Make sure small dog or puppy cannot get under it

Fence helps prevent dog from escaping

Make sure plants in your yard are not toxic for your dog

21 BASKETS & BEDDING

Most dog beds are cushioned fabric with a foam frame, wicker baskets, or plastic tublike beds. Also popular are beanbag beds, filled with polystyrene balls. Many fabric beds have zip-off washable covers. Wicker baskets and plastic tubs have certain advantages, but both can be a problem if your dog chews the corners. Your choice will be dictated by taste and availability in your dog's size.

Cushioned fabric dog bed

Wicker dog basket

THE PLASTIC OPTION
In theory, a plastic bed (lined with a blanket, pillow, or other soft base) is durable and chew-proof. It is also easier to wash clean than either a fabric or wicker bed.

22 FEEDING BOWLS

Each dog in your home should have its own food and water bowls. Stainless-steel ones are the most durable, and these usually come with a rubber ring attached to the bottom lip, to help prevent them from sliding across the floor while the dog eats. Ceramic bowls are heavier and less likely to slip around, but they are more prone to breakage if dropped.

Stainless-steel bowl   Ceramic bowl

GOOD HYGIENE
Keep food bowls clean, washing them between meals. Replace broken ceramic bowls, since bacteria can breed in the cracks.

23

COLLARS, LEASHES & HARNESSES

There is an enormous variety of choice in collars, leashes, and harnesses, and whatever you opt for will largely be dependent on the type and size of dog you have. Retractable leashes are great for small dogs that like to feel as though they are running free, whereas shorter metal chain leashes are tougher and ideal for larger, heavier dogs, literally keeping them on a short leash.

COLLARS
A collar should be wider than one of your dog's neck vertebrae. Attach an ID tag; rabies and license tags may be required as well.

Retractable leash

Lightweight nylon leash

Heavyweight nylon leash

Chain leash and leather collar

Lightweight nylon harness

COLLAR & LEASH
A standard collar-and-leash combination is suitable for most medium-size dogs, as well as some of the less boisterous large breeds.

BODY HARNESS
This harness goes over the dog's body and around its chest. It is designed to put no pressure on the delicate neck of a small dog.

19

24 SETTLING IN A NEW PUPPY

Allow the pup to have a look around the house, so that it knows its new environment. Take the first few days of your puppy's arrival at a slow pace, and be sure there is always one human family member around to keep watch over the dog and help it feel safe and secure.

CRATE EXPECTATIONS

If you intend to crate train your pup, use the crate from day one, so that the dog becomes accustomed to it.

25 SETTLING IN AN ADULT DOG

More often than not, this will be a rescue dog. You will probably visit it at the shelter several times before adopting it, allowing it to get used to you, and you will be given advice on how to behave when you bring it home. Adult dogs are, in some ways, easier to settle. Toilet training, for example, will probably be unnecessary.

COMFORTING TOUCH
An adult dog coming into your life may be disoriented, not knowing why a change of home has happened. Talk to it gently to relax it, but allow it to come to you for attention. When it does, comfort it with touches.

26 SETTLING IN A RESCUE DOG

Some rescue dogs have known behavioral problems and will require different house rules. For example, you may want to keep a dog that suffers from separation anxiety in a box beside your bed at night. Over time you should be able to move the box away, a little at a time, out of your room and into the room where you want the dog to sleep.

STAYING CLOSE
A rescue dog may not want to be alone on its first night in a new home. If it is stressed, allow it to sleep in a box next to your bed.

27 CHOOSING A NAME

The best name for a dog is something short, ideally with one or two syllables that can be said quickly, since this can be important at times—life and death, even. You will often have to call your dog's name in crowded parks or on the street, so choose something that will not cause any embarrassment. Avoid names that rhyme with a word used to control the dog—for example, Kit ("Sit").

WHAT'S IN A NAME?

If you have more than one pet (especially dogs and cats), aim to give them names that sound distinct from each other to avoid confusion among them.

Popular names for male dogs include: Sam, Jack, Ben, Spot, Rex, Max, Jake, Toby, Rocky, Marley, Charlie, Buddy, Eddie, Harley, Cody, Baxter, Teddy, Milo.

Popular names for female dogs include: Meg, Sue, Pip, Belle, Maisie, Lily, Rosie, Lulu, Missy, Molly, Piper, Roxy, Bailey, Sookie, Mia, Lady, Lucy Coco.

NAME TAG
Some people put a phone number on a dog tag instead of a name, since the latter makes it easier for a stranger to befriend the dog.

28 MICROCHIPPING YOUR DOG

It is sensible to have your dog microchipped, since a collar can be removed or may come unbuckled and fall off. Microchipping is a simple procedure in which a vet inserts a tiny electronic device under the skin in the neck. The codes on the chips are recognized internationally. In some countries and localities, it is required to have your dog microchipped.

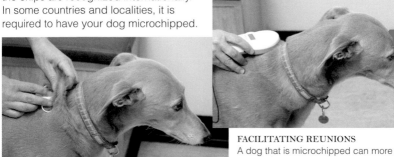

FACILITATING REUNIONS
A dog that is microchipped can more easily be returned home, since the chip contains a unique owner's code.

29 CHECKING YOUR DOG'S HEALTH

A healthy dog could be your companion for 10 years or more. If you are getting a puppy, choose carefully and spend some time with it observing its behavior before bringing it home. Consider the way it interacts with you and its siblings. Vitality and playfulness are important indicators of good health, as is an inquisitive attitude. The more you know your dog, the more alert you will be to any changes in its physical appearance or behavior that might indicate problems. There are also a few checks to help establish the overall well-being of a dog.

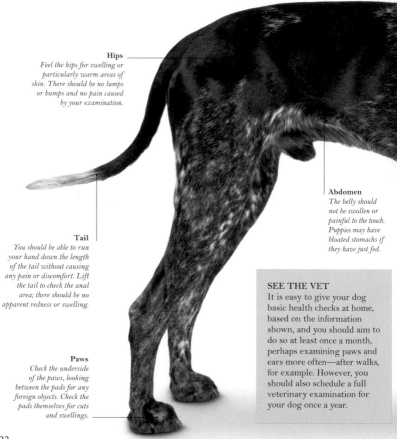

Hips
Feel the hips for swelling or particularly warm areas of skin. There should be no lumps or bumps and no pain caused by your examination.

Abdomen
The belly should not be swollen or painful to the touch. Puppies may have bloated stomachs if they have just fed.

Tail
You should be able to run your hand down the length of the tail without causing any pain or discomfort. Lift the tail to check the anal area; there should be no apparent redness or swelling.

Paws
Check the underside of the paws, looking between the pads for any foreign objects. Check the pads themselves for cuts and swellings.

SEE THE VET

It is easy to give your dog basic health checks at home, based on the information shown, and you should aim to do so at least once a month, perhaps examining paws and ears more often—after walks, for example. However, you should also schedule a full veterinary examination for your dog once a year.

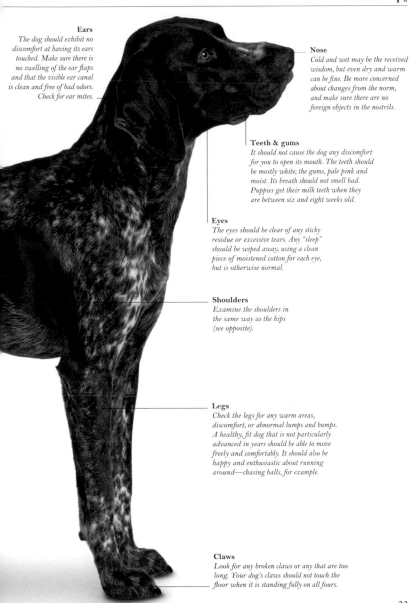

Ears

The dog should exhibit no discomfort at having its ears touched. Make sure there is no swelling of the ear flaps and that the visible ear canal is clean and free of bad odors. Check for ear mites.

Nose

Cold and wet may be the received wisdom, but even dry and warm can be fine. Be more concerned about changes from the norm, and make sure there are no foreign objects in the nostrils.

Teeth & gums

It should not cause the dog any discomfort for you to open its mouth. The teeth should be mostly white; the gums, pale pink and moist. Its breath should not smell bad. Puppies get their milk teeth when they are between six and eight weeks old.

Eyes

The eyes should be clear of any sticky residue or excessive tears. Any "sleep" should be wiped away, using a clean piece of moistened cotton for each eye, but is otherwise normal.

Shoulders

Examine the shoulders in the same way as the hips (see opposite).

Legs

Check the legs for any warm areas, discomfort, or abnormal lumps and bumps. A healthy, fit dog that is not particularly advanced in years should be able to move freely and comfortably. It should also be happy and enthusiastic about running around—chasing balls, for example.

Claws

Look for any broken claws or any that are too long. Your dog's claws should not touch the floor when it is standing fully on all fours.

Most vaccines are injected into scruff of neck

30 VACCINATIONS

The best way to prevent your dog from contracting diseases and parasites is to have it vaccinated. The first inoculations are given at around eight weeks of age. A puppy should not be in contact with unvaccinated dogs (that is, it should not be allowed outside) until it has had its first course of injections.

KEEP UP TO DATE

After the initial vaccinations, your dog will need regular boosters, especially if you want to travel abroad with it or put it in kennels.

31 VET CHECKUP

Take your dog for its first veterinary checkup as soon as possible after acquiring it. If you mention that you are bringing in an unvaccinated puppy, the vet will arrange for it not to come into contact with other dogs. You will be asked about the dog's background, if you know it. The vet will examine the dog, check its weight, microchip it, and give it its vaccinations.

Dog may need reassuring words while with vet

GOING FORWARD

Your vet will probably advise you on diet, flea control, neutering, and training, then give you an appointment for a follow-up visit.

32 NEUTERING

Most dog owners have their pet neutered to prevent unwanted pregnancies. Your vet will advise you on the best time to have this done, as well as what it involves. Dogs are rarely kept overnight after neutering. When you collect your dog, you will be given an Elizabethan collar (see p.64) to prevent your dog from licking its wounds. Analgesics and antibiotics are usually given by injection before the dog is discharged.

33 MEETING CHILDREN

Before introducing a new dog to children, warn them that, in a new environment, away from its siblings, the dog may be a little nervous at first. They should be quiet and wait for the dog to come to them. Give the children a few treats for the dog so that it might more readily approach them. Do not let the children grab at or pick up the dog on this first meeting; a nervous dog may scare easily and try to bite. Limit the time the kids and dog spend together so that neither gets overexcited.

PUPPY'S PACE
Allow a puppy to set the pace of early meetings with kids. Some are more outgoing than others.

FIRM FRIENDS
After a few meetings, once the new dog is comfortable with the children, they can be more hands-on in their playtime.

34 MEETING OLD PEOPLE

If your new puppy or adult dog is a little boisterous, exercise caution when introducing it to elderly members of the family, especially those who are unsteady on their feet. Start by asking the elderly person to sit rather than remain standing, and then allow the dog into the same room. Discourage the dog from trying to jump up, and allow it to approach the family member or friend in its own time, with some gentle encouragement along the way.

LAP DOG
Dogs of all sizes enjoy sitting on people's laps. Just be sure the person in question is comfortable with the arrangement.

TREAT TIME
Keep treats with you while out walking. You can give them to friendly strangers to help break the ice with your dog.

35 MEETING STRANGERS

Not every person your dog meets will be inside your house, so it is important that the new arrival is taught how to behave when encountering people out in the big wide world. When out walking, if your dog wants to approach strangers, allow it to do so while maintaining control of the leash. Bear in mind that some people are uncomfortable around dogs they don't know, so be sure to check before you approach them.

36 MEETING OTHER PETS

Restrain your new dog on its first meeting with other pets. You do not know how either will react, so limit how close they can get to each other. This is especially true with smaller animals that the dog might consider natural prey. It might be wise to put your dog or puppy in a crate when it meets a cat for the first time.

LIKE CAT & DOG
Cats may be wary on first meeting a new puppy. It is best to hold the dog back until the cat is comfortable around it.

DOG MEET DOG
Keep a close eye on adult dogs at their first meeting, especially if they are of the same sex.

37 SOCIALIZING

Contrary to the old adage, you can teach an old dog new tricks. Regardless of how old your new dog is, consider socialization classes to teach it how to behave around other dogs. This will make it much easier for you to control it while out walking, both on and off the leash. Your vet will be able to tell you who runs classes in your area.

MAKING FRIENDS
In many cases, dog encounters are perfectly harmless. They just want to learn about each other using their canine senses of touch and smell.

PUPPY CLASS
Training your puppy secures a better future for everyone. If your dog is not concerned with other dogs, it is less likely to get involved in fights.

38 VISITING NEW PLACES

After you have had your new dog vaccinated and microchipped, it is ready to be taken out on walks and exposed to new places and situations. It is important to start this as soon as possible with puppies, since it is part of the process of socialization. Dogs are far less accepting and more wary of new experiences after the age of 12 weeks.

RULES OF THE ROAD
Introduce your pup to traffic by sitting together at a safe distance from it. Reward calm behavior as cars go by with treats.

CARING FOR YOUR DOG

39 TYPES OF FOOD

Dog owners have a wide choice when it comes to deciding what to feed their canine companions. The important thing to remember is that food marketed for adult dogs is suitable for dogs aged nine months and over. Although prepared foods are convenient, the best way to know what your dog is eating is to create its meals yourself. Always adhere to the recommended food allowances for your pet (see Tip 43).

Manage your dog's diet

CANNED MOIST FOOD
Meaty canned dog food is a quick, easy choice, best served with dry supplements.

DRY FOOD
Crunchy dry foods come in two types: complete meal and snack foods.

SEMIMOIST FOOD
This type of food may contain high levels of sugar, so use it sparingly.

40 TABLE SCRAPS

It is important to discourage your dog from begging for whatever food you are eating. The best way to do this right from the beginning is never to feed it your leftovers directly from the table or wherever else you might be eating. If your uneaten food is suitable for your dog, put it into the dog's food bowl, and position the bowl in its usual place in the house.

Always use the dog's own bowl

41 PROVIDING ENOUGH WATER

Fresh water should be available for your dog at all times. Dogs lose water through their usual bodily functions—in urine and feces, as well as through panting—and that needs to be replenished. If a dog is unable to drink for 48 hours, it could suffer irreversible dehydration and organ damage. Fill the water bowl to the same level each day, so you can monitor how much your dog is drinking.

Always have clean water available

OUT AND AROUND

Take water out with you on walks. After running around, your dog will be thirsty and need fluids. Some dogs will drink from a bottle, but lightweight travel bowls are available, and many stores and restaurants will give water if asked.

KEEP IT CLEAN

Each time you refill your dog's water bowl, throw away any that is left over and wash the bowl thoroughly before reusing it.

42 SUITABLE TREATS & CHEWS

There are many types of branded treats available for your dog, and they can be great as rewards in training exercises. Do be aware, though, that—just like treats for humans—they can be high in fats, carbohydrates, and calories. An alternative to such treats are chews, which give a dog's teeth and gums a good workout, leave less mess around the house, and are far lower in calories. They can also keep a dog quiet for hours between walks.

GO EASY ON THE TREATS

If you use a lot of treats while training your dog, you should moderate its meal size to compensate.

43 HOW MUCH FOOD & WHEN?

The amount of food that you should give your dog will depend largely on its size, but also on its age and the amount of exercise it gets. Adult dogs—that is, those over nine months of age—may be fed their entire daily intake in one meal or it can be split into two meals; puppies need at least three meals a day for their first six months, dropping down to two between the ages of six and nine months.

DAILY FOOD REQUIREMENTS

Use this chart to help establish the correct portion sizes for your adult dog. Small dogs eat less in a single meal because of their smaller stomachs, so split their allowance over two meals.

Dog size: weight Breed example	Calories needed	Canned food/meal	Semimoist food	Dry food
Very small: 11 lb (5 kg) Yorkshire Terrier	210	3.7 oz (105 g) meat 1.2 oz (35 g) meal	2.5 oz (70 g)	2 oz (60 g)
Small: 22 lb (10 kg) Cairn Terrier	590	11 oz (300 g) meat 3.5 oz (100 g) meal	6.5 oz (190 g)	6 oz (170 g)
Medium: 44 lb (20 kg) Springer Spaniel	900	1 lb (450 g) meat 5.2 oz (150 g) meal	11 oz (300 g)	9 oz (260 g)
Large: 88 lb (40 kg) German Shepherd	1,680	2 lb (900 g) meat 10 oz (280 g) meal	1.2 lb (545 g)	1 lb (450 g)
Giant: 176 lb (80 kg) Great Dane	2,800	3 lb (1.4 kg) meat 1 lb (450 g) meal	2 lb (900 g)	1.7 lb (780 g)

44 SETTING A ROUTINE

To prevent any weight issues with your dog, do not leave food down at all times, and don't feed it whenever it comes looking around for something to eat. Choose feeding times that work for you in your work or home routine, and stick to them. Your dog will soon come to know exactly when its bowl will be filled.

DINNER O'CLOCK!

Set regular feeding times, and remove bowls when your dog has finished eating, especially if you are using moist or fresh foods.

45 FOODS TO AVOID

One good reason to make sure your dog does not steal food is that some foods that are suitable for humans can be hazardous for dogs. The consequences can range from mild stomach upsets to life-threatening illness or death.

AVOID CHOCOLATE
Human chocolate is poisonous for dogs. Use doggie chocs instead.

LIST OF FOODS
It is almost impossible to list every food that dogs should not eat. Here, though, is a selection of some of the most commonly available items that you should keep away from your dog.

• Chocolate • Coffee • Tea • Anything with caffeine • Apple cores • Mushrooms • Alcoholic drinks • Hops • Onions • Pits from peaches and plums • Fish • Grapes, raisins, and currants • Cat food • Tobacco • Salt • Raw eggs • Foods high in sugar • Rhubarb leaves • Avocado • Meat fats • Macadamia nuts • Milk and dairy products • Bread dough • Food that has spoiled or has developed mold.

46 DEALING WITH UNDERWEIGHT DOGS

A fit and healthy dog should be slim and muscular without being skinny. In most breeds, you should not be able to see the outlines of bones through the skin. If you are concerned about your dog being underweight, your vet can advise you on the right feeding regimen.

PUPPY WEIGHT
Find out the optimum weight for your dog, based on breed and gender, and work toward it with your vet's help.

Excess weight makes for unhealthy dogs

47 DEALING WITH OVERWEIGHT DOGS

Excess weight can lead to medical issues and shorten your dog's life. If your dog is overweight, speak to your vet. Your dog might have an underlying medical condition that causes weight gain or it might need more exercise.

FIGHTING THE FAT
Prevent obesity by feeding your dog according to daily requirements based on its breed and gender.

48 CLEANING EYES

Depending on the breed, you may find that your dog is prone to developing "sleep" in the corners of its eyes overnight. These crusty little balls are formed of normal discharge from the eye but should be removed each morning. In most cases, it is easy enough to wipe them away gently, using a clean piece of cotton for each eye. However, sleep can sometimes be stuck to the fur.

STUBBORN SLEEP
For particularly difficult bits of sleep, wipe the area gently with a cotton ball that has been moistened with lukewarm water.

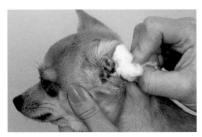

ANTISEPTIC EAR CLEANER
Wipe the insides of your dog's ear flaps with an antiseptic ear cleaner applied to a cotton ball. But do not push it into the ear canal.

49 CLEANING EARS

You should regularly examine your dog's ears for signs of redness, inflammation, discharge, and bad odors. The presence of any of these symptoms may be a sign of an infection, so see your vet as soon as you can. The same goes if you spot ear mites. A monthly cleaning regimen (see left) for the ears helps keep them healthy and goes a long way toward keeping infection at bay.

50 TRIMMING CLAWS

For most dogs, monthly claw-trimming should be adequate, but specific requirements will depend on the type of dog and its lifestyle. Cut the nails as close to the quick as possible, but take care not to cut the quick itself, since this will be painful for the dog. A cut quick will also bleed quite heavily and may, in worst-case scenarios, lead to infection.

CUTTING BLACK CLAWS
Black claws make it more difficult to see where the quick is. Remove small amounts at a time until you are happy with the length.

BATHING A DOG

51

Some dogs love being bathed and some don't. However, a bath is necessary from time to time to keep your dog's skin and coat free of parasites and to remove dirt (or whatever else it might have rolled in), odors, and any loose molting hair. Help make bath time more pleasurable by getting your dog used to it from a young age.

1 Gather everything you need within reaching distance: dog shampoo, a towel, and a brush. Lift your dog into the bath; use treats to calm it down if necessary.

2 After checking on your own hand that the water is warm but not too hot, wet the dog all over, working from head to tail, avoiding eyes, ears, and nose.

3 Apply dog shampoo and massage it well in, all over the coat, making sure you get all the way down to the skin. Once more, take care to avoid the eyes, ears, and nose.

5 Use your hands to squeeze any excess water from the coat, then towel your dog until almost dry. Finish off with a brush and, if possible, a hairdryer on a low setting.

4 Use warm water (again, first make sure it is not too hot) to rinse the dog's coat thoroughly of all shampoo. Any residue will cause irritation to the skin.

52 GROOMING EQUIPMENT

The grooming tools you need depend on the type of coat your dog has. Generally speaking, the longer the coat, the longer and wider the bristles of the brush. A professional groomer will be able to tell you which tools are right for your dog. Always clean your equipment after use to reduce the likelihood of contamination.

Rubber brush

Clippers   Slicker brush   Bristle brush   Chamois   Shedding blade   Fine comb   Coarse comb

53 SHEDDING

Dogs with smooth or shorthaired coats tend to shed their hair all year round, so they require regular brushing. Although curly and wiry coats molt less, they still need to be groomed regularly. Longhaired coats require attention every day to prevent tangling.

54 START EARLY

Accustom your dog to the grooming routine early in its life, as well as to the various grooming processes that will be necessary. If your dog has a heavy coat that will require regular clipping, for example, it needs to get used to the sound clippers make.

LEARNING CURVE
It takes practice to get the best results with clippers. Hold them lightly as you would a pencil, and keep the same angle throughout.

55 CLIPPING

Nonshedding, curly-coated dog breeds—Poodles, for example—need to be clipped. Many types of clipper are available, and clipper blades come with sized guard combs, determining the length to which the hair is cut. The best time to clip is after bathing and toweling your dog, so the coat is both clean and dry. Get advice from a groomer on how to clip your dog before attempting it yourself.

56 GROOMING SHORT COATS

All you need to do to keep a short-coated dog in perfect condition is a two-minute brush daily. Use a soft bristle brush for a smooth coat, and a firm bristle brush for a wiry coat. Once a week, carry out the slightly more involved session shown here. Stop using the shedding blade when it is difficult to remove more than half a brush-full of hair.

1 If your dog will tolerate it, use a hairdryer on a low setting to remove loose hair and dander from its coat.

Regular grooming leads to clean, odor-free coat

MINIMAL BATHING
If you groom your shorthaired dog regularly, you will only need to give it a bath occasionally.

2 Use a shedding blade to remove any remaining dead hair. Pass it lightly over the whole body in the direction of the hair.

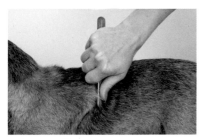

TOPCOAT GROOMING
The quickest way to hand strip is to use a hand-stripping knife. This removes the coarse topcoat from wire-haired breeds.

57 HAND STRIPPING

In this grooming method, hair is plucked from the root using a special tool. Most commonly, hand stripping is employed for certain wire-haired breeds, such as Border Terriers. The best time for hand stripping—and most comfortable for the dog—is when its coat is naturally shedding. As with clipping, ask a groomer for advice on hand stripping before doing it yourself.

58 GROOMING LONG COATS

Dogs with long coats need daily grooming to prevent the hair from tangling and matting. Occasional visits to a professional groomer will not be enough for dogs with long hair; you must attend to it yourself or risk your dog's coat becoming so bad that not only will the hair start to smell, but grooming will be painful for the dog. If your pet is not eager to be groomed, try doing it when the dog is relaxed or tired—after a long walk, for example.

1 If your dog's hair has become tangled, gently use a dematting comb first to break knotted hair into manageable sections.

2 After you have removed the big knots, use a slicker brush all over the coat to get rid of any tangles. Pay special attention to the feathering around the dog's legs.

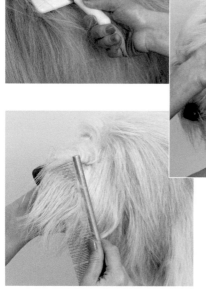

3 Next, use a rake brush or a medium bristle brush with long, wide-spaced bristles to work lightly through the coat from head to tail.

4 Finally, give the face some attention, combing the hair on the muzzle. Be especially careful with the comb's teeth around the eyes and nose.

59 GROOMING CURLY COATS

A lot of owners of curly-coated dogs prefer to take their pets to a professional groomer. However, much of the general upkeep of these coats can easily be done at home with very little effort. In addition to semiregular clipping (see Tip 55), these coats benefit from brushing and combing.

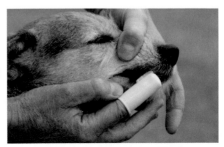

1 Work your way over the whole coat with a slicker brush, gently loosening up any snarls and knots and pulling out dead hair.

2 After brushing, use a comb to finish the job, untangling any stubborn knots and removing any leftover bits of dead hair.

60 BRUSHING YOUR DOG'S TEETH

Ideally, you should brush your dog's teeth once a week. First, get your dog used to the idea of having something put in its mouth. Do this by spending time resting your thumb across the bridge of its nose, with your fingers under the chin, keeping the mouth closed. After doing this a few times, use your other hand to gently lift the top lip to reveal the teeth. When the dog is used to this action, try to bring the toothbrush and paste into play. The most important area to brush is along the gum line, and you should work in a circular motion. Go at your dog's pace; you don't want to cause distress, since this will make it more difficult for future attempts. Only use dog-specific teeth-cleaning products.

A fingerbrush may be easier than a toothbrush.

37

LEARNING THE HOUSE RULES

61 EFFECTIVE DISCIPLINE

Dogs are pack animals that look up to a strong leader, and that should be you. It is important for your dog to understand this from the start, so have a set routine and stick to it. Your dog will learn faster if you are positive and consistent in what you expect from it. The training methods below will help you turn your dog into an obedient pet.

CHEWING
Puppies chew to ease the discomfort of teething. Supply your dog with chew toys to prevent this activity from turning destructive.

62 REWARDING GOOD BEHAVIOR

The easiest way to train a dog is by appealing to its innate desire to please and by using positive reinforcement rather than punishment. Reward and praise your dog when it behaves the way you want it to. It will soon learn to associate good behavior with rewards.

TREATS
Take a little time to find out what your dog craves. If it is motivated by food, reward its good behavior during a training session with a small, flavorful treat.

PRAISE
Words of praise and hugs are often reward enough for an eager-to-please dog and will reinforce the concept of good behavior.

USING HAND SIGNALS

63 It is easier for your dog to read your body language than it is to understand what you say, which makes hand signals a key element of its training. Make sure you have eye contact with your dog prior to giving any hand signals. Reinforce the visual signal with your voice; later, you can simply utter an instruction, and your dog will understand what to do. Praise your dog immediately if it does the right thing, so it associates action and reward.

Establish eye contact

Hand palm facing down

Face is relaxed

Arms are open and welcoming

SIT
This is one of the easiest commands for a dog to learn. Gently move your hand, palm up, toward your chest.

DOWN
Lure your dog into the down position with a treat. As soon as its elbows are on the floor, introduce the hand signal.

COME
At first, practice this hand signal over a short distance to ensure your dog's attention does not wander.

USING YOUR VOICE

64 Dogs can be trained to associate the sound of certain words with the actions they are expected to perform. Use short, one-word commands ("Sit," "Stay," "Fetch," and the like), and speak them clearly and with a cheerful, encouraging voice. Always use the same commands, and make sure that everyone else in the family does the same, to avoid confusing the dog.

EYE CONTACT
Establish eye contact with your dog prior to issuing a vocal instruction to ensure you have its full attention.

65 NEWSPAPER TRAINING

Take your puppy outside to relieve itself after meals and naps, and after exciting events such as meeting new people. Its behavior will also alert you to its need to relieve itself—if you see it sniffing and circling the same spot, take it outside. Until a toilet routine is established and adhered to, encourage your puppy to relieve itself on sheets of old newspaper.

Firm but gentle hold

Place dog on newspaper

Dog seeks reassurance that it is acting correctly

Paper is highly absorbent

1 When you see your puppy sniffing at the ground, pick it up and place it on newspaper. Stay with it until it relieves itself.

2 Praise your puppy for using the newspaper. Over time, regular toilet trips outside will be enough to avoid accidents indoors.

66 WHEN TOILET TRAINING FAILS

It is not always possible to keep an eye on your puppy, and accidents are bound to happen, especially in the early days. If your dog relieves itself indoors, do not reprimand it. Being scolded will only make your dog sneak to a place where it cannot be seen next time it is about to relieve itself, making it harder for you to prevent accidents by taking it outside or putting down some newspaper.

CLEANING UP
Clean the affected area with an ammonia-free disinfectant. It is vital to eliminate the smell, or your dog will use the same spot over and over again.

Accidents will happen

67 OUTDOOR TOILET TRAINING

Getting your dog used to an outdoor toilet routine is best done in conjunction with newspaper training (see Tip 65). The key to both types of toilet training is vigilance. Observe your dog for any behavior that might suggest it wants to relieve itself, and act accordingly. In the meantime, aim to establish regular outside toileting times.

1 If your dog starts sniffing the ground and circling the same spot, it might be looking for a spot in which to relieve itself.

2 Act quickly to prevent an accident. Take your dog out into the yard or for a walk so it can relieve itself in an appropriate spot.

3 If you are letting your dog out into the yard, go with it and stay until it has relieved itself. Then praise it for doing it outside.

SAFE HAVEN
Get your puppy accustomed to spending quiet time in a crate, and as it grows up, it will come to see it as a safe place at busy or stressful times.

68 CRATE TRAINING

Get your puppy used to spending its quiet time in a crate. Make sure the crate is equipped with everything your dog might need: soft bedding, a chew toy or a food-releasing toy, a water bowl, and a newspaper for toileting. Place the crate in the room where you will be spending time—for example, the kitchen while you are preparing food. At first, leave your puppy in the crate for no longer than 30 minutes or so; over time, you will be able to increase the length of its stay. Never use crate time as a form of punishment.

41

69 TEACHING A DOG ITS NAME

It is important to teach your dog to recognize its own name and to come back to you when it is called. When your dog learns this, you can start letting it off the leash on walks where permitted. Train your dog to come when called in an environment that is familiar to it and where there are few distractions, such as an enclosed backyard. You might have to recruit a friend or another family member to help the first few times.

1 Ask a friend to restrain your dog gently but firmly by the collar, then allow it to sniff a tasty treat. Do not give the treat.

2 Take the treat and move about 10ft (3m) away from your dog. Squat down. Open your arms wide to indicate "Come" (see Tip 63) and call your dog's name.

3 Instruct your friend to release your dog as soon as you call its name. Keep your arms open to encourage your dog to come to you.

4 When your dog is near you, lure it closer still by giving it the treat you had promised. Gently hold it by the collar and praise it, repeating its name.

70 TEACHING TO SIT

Teaching your dog to sit when asked will allow you to have control over it at times of excitement—for example, when you have visitors. As with all dog-training exercises, practice when your dog is relaxed and in a place with few distractions. You can use your voice or your hand, or a combination of both (see p.39).

1 Stand in front of your dog with a treat in your hand. Allow it to smell your hand, then slowly move the treat over its head.

2 This action will force your dog to lift its nose and move backward into a sitting position. Say "Sit." When your dog does, release the treat and praise it.

71 TEACHING TO SIT & STAY

This instruction is particularly useful to control your dog in potentially dangerous situations—for example, when the front door is left open to allow for deliveries or a large number of people to come in. It is a good idea to train your dog to sit and stay when it is feeling tired, since it will then be more likely to want to stay in one position.

1 Instruct your dog to sit (see Tip 70), then get it to remain in the sitting position by bringing your hand down slowly toward its face.

2 Reward your dog by bringing a treat to its level. Repeat steps 1 and 2, leaving it longer between instruction and reward.

3 Your dog will eventually learn to wait for a minute or longer. At this stage, move away slightly. Reward your dog if it stays seated.

72 TEACHING TO WALK TO HEEL

By teaching your pup to walk on a loose leash and, ultimately, to heel, you lay the foundations for pleasurable dog-walking in the years to come. One of the most important things to bear in mind during this training is not to pull on the leash. You should aim to encourage the dog to be near you because it wants to be, not because it has no other choice or is unable to move away from you.

1 With the handle of the leash in your right hand and a treat in your left, encourage the pup to follow the treat behind you until it stands next to your left leg. Reward with the treat.

2 Place another treat near your dog's nose, then draw it away to keep its attention on you and its gaze upward. Speak the pup's name and say "Heel."

3 Move forward one step. Give the treat and enthusiastic praise if the dog moves with you. This encourages further obedience.

4 Increase the number of steps you take between rewards. Begin each new training session with the same one-step reward to refresh the dog's memory.

73 TEACHING TO LIE DOWN

Teaching your puppy to lie down is a very effective way of taking control of situations in which the dog becomes overly excited. It also helps develop the dog's self-control, since it will learn that this position must be maintained even if running around seems like more fun. Be patient when teaching lying down, and continue to practice until the dog responds immediately to you saying "Down" under all circumstances.

1 Start by asking your dog to sit (see Tip 70). Use a treat near its nose to lead the pup down. Allow the dog to lick at the reward but not eat the whole thing.

2 Move the treat toward the ground to lure the puppy down. Say "Down" as you keep allowing access to the treat. If the dog tries to get up, go back to the sit position.

3 When both of the dog's elbows are on the ground, give the rest of the treat and enthusiastic praise. Be patient—it will become easier in future attempts.

74 TEACHING TO GIVE ITEMS

There will be times when you want your dog to let go of something it has in its mouth. In most cases, it will be a ball or similar toy that you need to be able to throw again so the fun can continue. However, it is also a useful skill should the dog pick up an item that is toxic or could cause injury.

FROM MOUTH TO HAND
Use fetch time to teach giving. Place your hand under the dog's chin in readiness to catch the ball, then use the instruction "Give." Aim to have the ball delivered into your hand; if the dog misses, try again until your puppy gets it right.

75 DEALING WITH EXCESSIVE BARKING

Dogs bark for several reasons: when they are bored, because they want attention, or to alert us to something. Barking due to separation anxiety or for attention needs to be dealt with. Your dog must learn that to have your attention it must behave. Ignore the dog when it barks, then do some simple training exercises, such as asking it to sit or lie down. Only give it a reward when it is quiet.

Excessive barking can frustrate family and annoy neighbors

BARK CONTROL
If a dog is particularly obedient, you may be able to control its barking with instructions such as "Speak" and "Quiet."

76 DEALING WITH AGGRESSION

Most aggressive behavior is likely to be between male dogs. Neutering at a young age can help reduce such behavior, but watch for body-language indicators while walking off-leash. This is where "Come" training (see Tip 69) is invaluable, but distract the dog with a favorite toy and treat, too.

TO OTHER DOGS
Much of what seems like aggression between dogs is simply defensive behavior.

TO PEOPLE
If your dog is aggressive toward people, you will need to ask a professional dog trainer for help.

77 BEGGING & STEALING FOOD

The most effective way of preventing your dog from begging and stealing food is not to let the opportunity present itself. Additionally, though, feed your dog only from its own bowl and always in the same place. In the event of these behaviors occurring, give a firm "Leave" command. Of course, there will be times when food is in a position that makes it easy to steal. Be sure to praise and reward your dog when it does not take advantage of such situations.

BEGGING

Begging can be prevented early in life by refusing to feed your dog from your plate or table. Feed the dog well away from your own eating area.

STEALING

Dogs are easily tempted, so try not to leave food unattended. If your dog steals from the garbage can, use one with a lid that closes tightly, and make sure that it never overflows.

Unattended food is very tempting to many dogs

TIME FOR FUN & EXERCISE

78 HOW MUCH EXERCISE?

Even the smallest dogs should be taken out for a walk at least once a day. Keep it on a leash where regulations dictate, but if you have trained it to come back when called, remove the leash for an untethered run. Since you are out anyway, why not take a ball and play fetch for a good exercise session even when time is short?

SWEET FREEDOM
Dogs can run faster than people, so in order to exercise them to the full, allow them to run free and explore off the leash.

79 SET A ROUTINE

It's good for you and it's good for your dog to have a fixed routine for walks and playtime. That way you can hope to avoid the randomness of requests from your canine pal, because its body clock will set itself according to the times you set.

COME RAIN OR SHINE
Sticking to a schedule makes it easier for everyone—dogs included. Just hope for good weather!

80 COMBATING DOG BOREDOM

We can't all be at our dog's beck and call every minute the day, so there are times when it will feel ignored or bored. If you have to be out of the home for many hours, take the dog out for a walk first, to burn up any excess energy, and leave some food. Making its food less accessible—for example, by stuffing a kong—also helps occupy a dog's time.

LOOKING FOR FUN
Dogs need a stimulating environment and interaction with humans or other animals to keep boredom at bay.

PUPPY PLAYTIME
Keep your puppy entertained while outdoors by providing it with a toy and interacting with it.

81 PUPPY'S FIRST TIME OUTSIDE

For the first few months of their lives, most pups will live indoors, although they should ideally have supervised access to a yard or similarly enclosed outdoor space from just a few weeks old. Part of your pup's training should involve being taken outside first thing in the morning and after meals, just long enough for it to do its toilet duties. Only leave a puppy alone outside if it is in a safe environment, such as a dog run, and even then, only for short periods of time.

PLAYING WITH FOOD
Combine snacks and fun by giving your dog a hollow chew toy that is designed to have dog food stuffed inside it.

THE HUMAN TOUCH
Get your dog accustomed to playing gently with people. Allow it to sniff and touch you, but draw the line at mouthing or biting.

82 LEASHES & CONTROL

If you let your puppy pull on the leash, you will end up with a stronger adult dog that will do the same. Consider the leash as a guide rather than a restraint. Keep it loose and, instead, rely on vocal instructions (see Tip 64). Teach your dog to walk to heel (see Tip 72), and use the leash as a restraint only when it is necessary for reasons of safety.

If a dog pulls on the leash, you have lost control of it

SPACE TO ROAM
Keep your hands at your side and allow your dog space to roam. Anticipate its actions, shortening the leash as needed.

OUT OF CONTROL
Avoid tug-of-war with the leash by distracting your dog and removing it from any tense situations before it is even aware of them.

POOP THEN PLAY
Once you have cleaned up after your dog, let it off the leash. It will soon learn that playtime comes after toilet time.

83 POOP SCOOPING

The simple act of going for a walk will stimulate your dog's need to poop. It will probably happen very early into the walk, so keep your dog on the leash until it has done its business. Carry biodegradable poop bags with you whenever you take your dog for a walk; rolls of bags can be placed in poop-bag dispensers that may be hooked onto a belt or to the handle of the leash. In some places, owners are legally required to clean up after their dogs.

Look out for no-poop zones

84

SUITABLE TOYS

Buy good-quality dog toys from reputable stores so you can be sure that they meet all relevant safety standards. Opt for toys that are suitable to the size and age of your pet—do not buy balls that are so small that they might be a choking hazard, for example. Reduce the chance of possessiveness and aggression developing in your dog by limiting its time with any one toy, and put toys away out of sight when playtime is over.

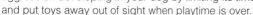

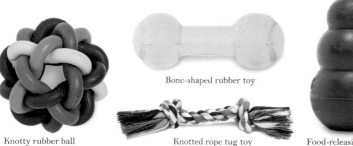

Bone-shaped rubber toy

Knotty rubber ball

Knotted rope tug toy

Food-releasing toy

Dog pull

Rope and balls tug toy

THE RIGHT STUFF

Only use real dog toys with your pet. If you use old shoes or clothes, it sends the message that chewing shoes and clothes is acceptable.

Balls provide hours of fun with very little need for human interaction

85 GAMES TO PLAY

There are hundreds of games you can play with your canine companion—the most important thing is to keep the dog active, both physically and mentally. Tennis balls and Frisbees are great fun for playtime and cost just pennies; or you can spend considerably more for agility or flyball equipment (see opposite).

CATCH
A standard tennis ball is perfect for catch, or you can buy a hollow rubber ball that has a little more bounce to keep your dog off guard a little.

FETCH
This game can be made easier on the arm by buying adapted balls with rope handles or a throwing stick. Your dog will get plenty of physical exercise with this activity.

Two dogs can play tug-of-war together if supervised

TUG-OF-WAR
Once your dog has learned to give items on command (see Tip 74), you can play tug-of-war games. This is a good way to release any excess energy that may have built up after having been left alone for a few hours.

FRISBEE

The way a Frisbee glides through the air means that a good throw gives your dog the time to try to get under it and catch it before it hits the ground. Make sure you have plenty of open space for this game.

FIELD TRIALS

Gundog breeds such as Spaniels, Setters, and Pointers enjoy searching for toys and then retrieving them.

AGILITY

This type of training requires excellent dog-handling skills. The best advice is to join a club and learn from an expert. At the outset of any agility training, walk through the course with your dog on a leash.

FLYBALL

In flyball, the dog is expected to put its weight on a mechanism that releases a ball, which should then be caught. If you want your dog to learn this activity, join a special club.

86 TRAVELING IN A CAR

The best way to get your dog accustomed to going on long trips in the car is to take it for several regular short trips before attempting any long ones. Avoid feeding before starting out, to reduce the likelihood of vomiting, and carry a large plastic container of water. If you are on a very long drive, take toilet breaks every couple of hours at least, and also allow the dog a little exercise and some water.

TRAVELING IN COMFORT
The safest way for a dog to travel is inside a crate in the hatchback part of the car. Line the crate with a small blanket or sheepskin rug so your dog can lie down in comfort.

SUITABLE RESTRAINT
In many areas, dogs must be "suitably restrained" when traveling in a car. If you don't own or have room for a crate, consider a seatbelt harness.

87 PREVENTING OVERHEATING

Install sunshades on your car windows to keep the sun off your dog while traveling. Not only will this keep your dog cool, but it will also help to reduce the risk of overexcitement at the passing scenery. Never leave a dog unattended in a car in warm weather, or in cool weather with the heat running. It is not even safe to park in a shaded area with the window open. If you leave the car, take the dog with you.

HOT DOG
Dogs are not very well able to control their body temperatures. If they overheat, they may suffer potentially fatal heatstroke.

88 BOARDING AT KENNELS

It is not always possible to take your dog with you when you go away, and you will need to consider its care in your absence. A popular option is boarding kennels. Your vet should be able to recommend good ones in your area. Visit several kennels before choosing the one that is right for you, based on facilities and your impression of the premises and owner. Before a long trip, leave your dog overnight on a couple of occasions to get it used to the different environment.

ASKING THE RIGHT QUESTIONS
Check that any kennels have the right licenses, will stick to your feeding schedules, will handle and exercise your dog, and can offer access to 24-hour veterinary care.

USING DOG SITTERS
Most people prefer to leave their dog in the care of friends or family. The best scenario is for your dog to move into that person's home rather than to leave the dog alone in yours. To help ensure this works smoothly, visit the vacation home several times in advance, so your dog knows the place and people involved. Leave plenty of your dog's favorite food with the sitter, along with details of exercise, eating, and sleeping routines. If you opt for a registered sitter, get suggestions from your vet or other dog owners, and ask the sitter for references.

Meeting the pet sitter

BOOK EARLY
The most personal boarding kennels often have limited space, so it is wise to book as far in advance as possible once you find one you are happy with.

YOUR DOG'S HEALTH

89 SIGNS OF GOOD HEALTH

Although it is advisable to take your dog to the vet once a year for a medical checkup and annual rabies vaccination (which is required to license your dog), you should also carry out regular observations of your own, paying special attention to those areas shown below, where problems most commonly occur. Some routine maintenance can be carried out at home (see Tip 29), but visit your vet if you are unsure about anything you find during your regular checkups.

ANAL AREA
This area should be clean and free of malodorous secretions. Keep an eye out for blocked anal sacs, or white grains that indicate worms.

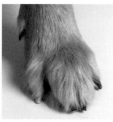

FEET
The paw pads should be free of cuts and burns. Make sure there are no broken or damaged claws.

EYES

Your dog's eyes should be bright and clear, so look for any squinting or wateriness. See your vet if any problems have not cleared within a day.

EARS

The inside of the ears should be pink, with no discharge or odor. Head shaking may indicate ear problems.

MOUTH

The teeth should be white; the gums, pink. Check for bad breath, chipped teeth, and inflamed gums

SKIN

The skin should be free of inflammation and flakiness. Signs of skin issues include hair loss, but also scratching, chewing, and licking.

90 CONTROLLING PARASITES

Treat your dog for fleas regularly, especially during the warm summer months. Since fleas can survive away from the dog, it is also important to treat the home environment. Ticks are blood-sucking parasites that latch onto your dog's skin, especially around the face. Get your dog used to having its head checked for ticks after walks, especially in tall grass. Worms are internal parasites that can live in the lungs, the intestines, or the heart; the best preventive measure is a worming pill every six months.

FLEAS & TICKS

Symptom: If your dog scratches a lot, it might have fleas. Part its coat so you can see the skin. Fleas look like tiny brown specks, but the presence of small black droppings is also a sign of an infestation, as is red, irritated skin. Ticks look and feel like small warts on your dog's skin.

Treatments: Flea treatment is available in the form of several products that are applied to the back of your dog's neck; your home and other pets should also be treated. Ticks must be removed manually; it is a tricky task, so ask your vet to explain how.

Excessive scratching

EAR MITES

Symptom: Persistent scratching of and pawing at the ears and vigorous shaking of the head are usually symptomatic of an ear-mite infestation. Check the inside of your dog's ears for the presence of dark spots and brown waxy discharge. There might also be an unpleasant smell.

Treatments: Some topical flea-treatment products are also effective in the elimination of mites. Consult your vet for further advice. In the case of severe infestations, your vet may prescribe drops.

Pawing at the ears

WORMS

Symptom: There are different symptoms for different types of worm. The lungworm causes breathing problems, such as a persistent cough, while worms that take up residence in your dog's intestines might cause weight loss, diarrhea, and anemia, which reveals itself as pale gums. Worms might also be visible in your dog's stools.

Treatments: Dogs should be wormed regularly for intestinal roundworms and tapeworms. Your vet will be able to advise as to the most suitable treatment.

Licking the rear end

91 SIGNS OF DISTRESS & PAIN

The more you get to know your dog, the easier it will be to determine what is normal, what is unusual, and whether it is in any pain or distress. Early detection is important, so learn to recognize the signs of canine ill health—even a seemingly innocuous change in your dog's physical appearance or behavior could be an indication that something is not right. When you spot anything out of the ordinary, make an appointment with your vet. It is better to be safe than sorry.

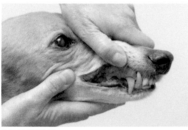

APPETITE
Whether your dog isn't eating its food or has developed a voracious appetite, it is always wise to investigate any changes in its eating habits.

PALE GUMS
Your dog's gums speak volumes about its overall health. If they look pale, your dog could have anemia or be in shock.

PANTING
It is normal for a dog to pant, especially after exercising. However, excessive panting can indicate overheating or other conditions, such as pneumonia or heartworm. Contact your vet for advice.

LIFTING A LEG
If your dog is keeping a paw off the ground, check it for lacerations or foreign objects stuck in it. Lifting a leg can also be a sign of muscular, joint, or bone problems.

EXCESSIVE LICKING
If your dog is licking obsessively, it might be trying to ease its pain or discomfort. Check the area for open wounds. Licking can also be indicative of stress and anxiety.

92 TENDING TO SMALL WOUNDS

If your dog suffers a small, clean wound, you may decide to deal with it yourself rather than call the vet. Irrigate the wound with a saline solution (you can make this at home by dissolving 1 teaspoon of salt in 2 cups of water), then carefully trim the hair around the wound. Apply a sterile bandage and put your dog in an Elizabethan collar to prevent it from bothering the wound.

BANDAGING A PAW
Apply some sterile dressing to the wound and secure it by wrapping a bandage around it. It should be tight without causing discomfort.

93 TENDING TO STINGS

Curious dogs may try to chase bees and wasps, and end up getting stung in the process. The most common site for stings is the face. If your dog's face displays an unusual swelling, look for a sting and, if you can, remove it with tweezers. Some dogs are allergic to stings. If your dog develops breathing difficulties, take it to the vet at once.

Beware of bee stings

94 TENDING TO BITES

When dogs fight one another, they tend to bite the area around the muzzle, the ears, and the neck. If your dog gets into a fight, break it up by throwing water at them. Next, wait until your dog has calmed down before examining it for bites. If you see a puncture wound or a laceration, take it to your vet at once. Penetrative wounds can often become infected, and your dog will have to start a course of antibiotics.

EAR WOUNDS
Dogs' ears will bleed heavily from the tiniest cut. A vet will treat the injury and bandage the ear to the head to keep it immobile.

95

WHEN TO GO TO THE VET

Learning to read the signs of ill health in your dog will prevent unnecessary trips to the vet, which can be stressful for your canine companion, as well as expensive for you. However, do not hesitate to consult your vet if your dog has a persistent complaint, any visible injuries, or if it appears to be in shock or pain. Serious problems may be prevented by the early treatment of some symptoms.

CHOOSING A VET

The best way to find a vet is by word of mouth. Ask your friends and neighbors where they take their pets, and whether they are happy with the care they receive there. You can also ask your local rescue shelter where they take their residents for checkups.

At the clinic, ask about their facilities and whether they provide around-the-clock emergency care. Also find out how many vets practice there and whether your dog will see the same one each time.

PET INSURANCE

Veterinary emergencies are expensive affairs. In addition to the cost of treatment, you may have to consider the cost of kenneling, since an injured dog might need to stay in overnight for observation.

In order to face these bills, it is wise to insure your dog. You will still have to pay your vet upfront, but after filing a claim form, you should get a large portion of the money spent on the treatment back.

CONFIDENT HANDLING

A visit to the vet does not have to be a fearful experience for your dog. Vets can put it at ease with a few hugs, a soothing voice, and reassuring body language.

96 CARING FOR A PREGNANT DOG

Dog pregnancies last about two months and become visible just after the halfway mark. If your dog is expecting puppies, she will need extra attention in terms of health care, diet, and exercise. Ask your vet to examine your dog and confirm that she is healthy and free of parasites. As she approaches mid-term, your dog will require increased quantities of food. She is also likely to start preferring short, more frequent forays outside rather than long walks that take her far from home.

PHYSICAL CHANGES
As your dog's pregnancy progresses, you will start to notice changes in the size of her abdomen and a darkening of her nipples.

WHELPING BOX
Prepare a whelping box lined with a soft blanket in a quiet area of the house. Be prepared to spend some time in it with your dog to show her that it is a safe place.

Front of whelping box can be raised or lowered

Pregnant dogs have a greater appetite

Newspaper is excellent nesting material

NUTRITION
Growing healthy pups and producing milk require a lot of energy. Make sure your pregnant dog's diet in the run-up to delivery meets all her nutritional needs.

NESTING
If you see your pregnant dog gathering nesting material, such as newspaper, gently encourage her into the whelping box you have prepared for her.

97 CARING FOR AN ELDERLY DOG

As your dog grows older, it will start displaying age-related ailments, such as stiff joints, arthritis, diminished sight and hearing, lethargy, and sometimes senile behavior. However, you can do a lot to alleviate these symptoms and enable your dog to enjoy its senior years. Being observant is key. Be alert to any difficulty your dog might display, and act to ease its discomfort. Keep it warm; feed it a good, healthy diet; and continue to give it gentle daily walks.

KEEPING WARM
Elderly dogs are not able to regulate their body temperature as well as their younger counterparts. When you go out for a walk, make sure your dog has a warm coat.

HELPING HAND
Jumping into the back of the car might not come so easy to an aging dog. Pick it up or teach it to use a ramp when heights are involved.

WEIGHT CONTROL
Help your dog enjoy its old age by keeping its weight under control. Maintaining a healthy weight will be kinder on your dog's joints.

Ergonomic raised food bowl

EATING AID FOR LARGE DOGS
As your dog ages and its joints become stiffer, you might want to help it at mealtimes by providing it with a raised food bowl. Eating this way will also aid your dog's digestion.

98

CARING FOR A SICK DOG

If your dog is recovering from a bout of illness or from any type of surgery, you will have to pay extra care to its needs. Your vet will be able to advise you on the specifics, but in general, a sick dog should be kept comfortable and warm. Invest in an Elizabethan collar to prevent it from bothering wounds or stitches. Allow your dog to take things easy until it feels better, with shorter walks and less excitement than usual.

REST IS IMPORTANT
After taking your dog home from the vet, prepare a cozy bed for it using a soft cushion or a warm blanket. Place the bed in a quiet area of the house and allow your dog to sleep it off.

GIVING MEDICINE
The easiest way to give your dog its medicine is by hiding it in its food—provided the medicine does not have to be taken on an empty stomach. If the medicine is liquid, squirt it in your dog's bowl, mixing it with its food; if it is in pill form, wrap it in some meat or bread.

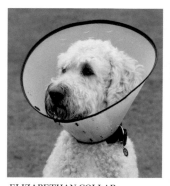

ELIZABETHAN COLLAR
Ensure your dog does not lick a sore spot or bother its stitches by putting it in a collar. You may have to remove it to allow your dog to eat and drink.

99 GIVING PILLS & LIQUID MEDICINE

If the directions for use say that a certain medication should be taken on an empty stomach, you will not be able to hide it in your dog's food (see opposite). Some dogs are more amenable than others to being given medicine by mouth; if yours is reluctant to cooperate, immobilize it by holding it firmly between your legs. If giving your dog a pill proves to be impossible, ask the vet whether the medication is also available in liquid form, since it is often easier to administer with the help of a syringe.

LIQUID MEDICINE

It is easier to administer liquid medicine to a dog, because its mouth does not have to be fully open. Fill a syringe with the correct amount of medication, then hold your dog's head still. Do not tilt it upward. Insert the syringe into the corner of your dog's mouth and squirt its contents between its cheek and teeth. Reward your dog.

Using a syringe to give liquid medication

1 Get your dog to sit. Gently but firmly open its mouth, tilting its head backward. Drop the pill into the back of its throat.

2 Close your dog's mouth and keep it closed while massaging the pill down its throat. Give your dog plenty of praise.

100 SYMPTOMS OF ILL HEALTH

Although dogs cannot tell us what is wrong with them, their bodies and their behavior speak volumes about their state of health. People who share their life with a dog will soon get to know what constitutes normal behavior for their canine companion and what is unusual. Keep an eye out for any changes in their appetite, energy levels, and habits. At least once a week, examine their mouth, ears, and eyes, and check their breath. If anything seems out of the ordinary, consider a trip to the vet.

SCRATCHING
Persistent scratching is probably related to the presence of fleas, ear mites, or other parasites. Check your dog's coat and ears for uninvited guests.

LETHARGY
Dogs are easily stimulated by their environment, so a lack of interest in everything is a definite cause for concern, especially if it is accompanied by loss of appetite.

POSSIBLE PARASITES
A dog that constantly bites and licks at its rear end may have worms or anal-sac irritation. The latter is more likely if it also displays scooting behavior, dragging its bottom along the floor.

CHANGES IN EATING HABITS
Monitor your dog's appetite, since any changes could be signs of ill health. If your dog refuses to eat for more than 24 hours, especially if it shows no interest even in its favorite foods, consult the vet.

URINARY TRACT PROBLEMS
Changes in the frequency and quantity of urination may be causes for concern. If your dog produces only a few drops of urine or, conversely, if it is urinating large amounts, see your vet as soon as possible.

BEHAVIORAL CHANGES
If your dog suddenly displays unusual behavior—snapping when it has always been docile, for example—it might be in pain, or there might be something wrong.

LIST OF OTHER SYMPTOMS

If you are worried about any aspect of your dog's health, call your vet for advice. You may be asked to take the dog in. Here are some symptoms you might encounter.

• **Altered breathing pattern or unusual sounds while breathing** are indicators of respiratory disorders.

• **Coughing or sneezing** may simply be allergic reactions but could also be responses to foreign bodies lodged in the nose or the ingestion of toxic substances.

• **Distress while urinating or defecating** may indicate digestive system disorders.

• **Open wounds** should not be left untreated, since they may become infected.

• **Waekness, limping, or stiffness in joints** are cause for concern in young, otherwise healthy dogs.

• **Reduced appetite** can be symptomatic of a digestive disorder.

• **Sudden excessive hair loss** can be an extreme reaction to parasites on the coat or a symptom of a hormonal disorder.

• **Persistent scratching** is commonly associated with fleas, ticks, or mites.

• **Increased thirst** may indicate the onset of a hormonal disorder such as diabetes or Cushing's syndrome.

Sudden snapping or growling may indicate something as serious as brain tumor

101 COMMON CANINE COMPLAINTS

There are myriad ailments, illnesses, and complaints that can affect a dog's various body parts. Some are caught from other dogs, while others might be common to certain breeds. The key to the best treatment is to spot issues early. This can best be facilitated through routine handling and checking of your dog, and by knowing what feels and looks normal for it.

Cavalier King Charles Spaniels are prone to heart disease

JOINTS

Joint disease can be so mild as to go unnoticed by a pet owner or, at the other extreme, it can greatly affect an animal's life. Most cases fall somewhere between the two.

PROBLEM SIGNS
• Limping • Stiffness • Inability to jump • Lack of desire to move • Difficulty climbing stairs • Favoring one leg over another • Displaying signs of discomfort or pain when moving

EYES

Among the most common eye problems are corneal injuries due to fighting or scratching the eye when sniffing around bushes. Check your dog's eyes regularly to ensure all is well.

PROBLEM SIGNS
• Redness • Swelling • Presence of discharge • Cloudiness • Wateriness • Opacity of the lens • Bulging eyes • Tear-stained fur around eyes • Inflamed cornea • Visible third eyelid

EARS

Infections of the ear can be uncomfortable and should be treated quickly. Ear mites are common and contagious, so treat all your pets at the first sign of infestation.

PROBLEM SIGNS
• Tilted head • Head shaking • Redness/swelling • Unpleasant odor • Pawing/scratching ear area • Loss of balance • Sensitive near ears • Discharge • Dark brown wax • Hearing loss • Bleeding

SKIN & HAIR

A wide range of problems can affect a dog's skin and hair, including bacterial infections, yeast infections, fleas and lice, ringworm, allergic dermatitis, and even alopecia.

PROBLEM SIGNS

• Constant scratching or licking • Hair loss • Blotchy or red skin • Spots around chin • Red ear flap • Lesions • Chewing obsessively at reachable extremities • Black dust in fur • Flaky skin

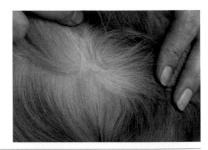

DIGESTIVE SYSTEM

There are many ailments that can strike at the digestive system. Some of the most common are intestinal obstruction, food poisoning, and anal-sac irritation.

PROBLEM SIGNS

• Diarrhea • Vomiting • Frequent regurgitation • Constipation • Distended belly • Loss of appetite • Obsessive cleaning of anal area • Weight loss • Increased frequency of defecation

RESPIRATORY SYSTEM

Kennel cough is serious and contagious, but preventive vaccination is possible. Any coughs or sneezes should be investigated, especially if persistent, because foreign bodies may be present in the nose or throat.

PROBLEM SIGNS

• Wheezing • Coughing • Sneezing • Choking • Gagging • Rapid, shallow breathing • Noisy breathing • Difficulty breathing

HEART & BLOOD

From heart disease and blood clots, to thyroid problems and anemia (which may indicate underlying concerns), there is no shortage of issues that can affect a dog's circulatory system. See a vet if you are concerned.

PROBLEM SIGNS

• Lethargy and weakness • Weight loss • Diminished appetite • Fever • Depression • Increased heart rate

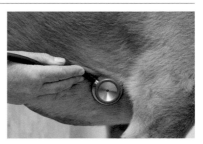

INDEX

ACKNOWLEDGMENTS

Sands Publishing Solutions would like to thank
Kim Bryan for her efficient consultancy work during the project,
as well as for her assistance in fine-tuning the contents at the outset;
Natalie Godwin for design assistance; and the ever-brilliant Hilary Bird
for making such swift work of the index.

Dorling Kindersley would like to thank the following photographers:
Gerard Brown, Jane Burton, Andy Crawford, Dave King, Steve Lyne, Ray Moller,
David Morgan, Tracy Morgan, Gary Ombler, Tim Ridley, Steve Shott, David Ward.

Picture credits
10 tl: Peter Kirillov © Fotolia.
39 tl, tc, tr: Simon Murrell.
52 br: puppy courtesy of Suzanne and Molly.
53 tl: Peter Kirillov © Fotolia.
64 tr: puppy courtesy of Richbourne Kennels.

All other images © Dorling Kindersley.
For further information, see www.dkimages.com

COMBOGUARD®
(spinosad + milbemycin oxime)
Chewable Tablets

Caution: Federal (USA) law restricts this drug to use by or on the order of a licensed veterinarian.

Description: COMBOGUARD (spinosad and milbemycin oxime) is available in five sizes for oral administration to dogs and puppies according to their weight. Each chewable flavored tablet is formulated to provide a minimum spinosad dose of 13.5 mg/lb (30 mg/kg) and a minimum milbemycin oxime dose of 0.2 mg/lb (0.5 mg/kg). Spinosad is a member of the spinosyns class of insecticides, which are non-antibacterial tetracyclic macrolides. Spinosad contains two major factors, spinosyn A and spinosyn D, derived from the naturally occurring bacterium, *Saccharopolyspora spinosa*. Spinosyn A and spinosyn D have the chemical compositions $C_{41}H_{65}NO_{10}$ and $C_{42}H_{67}NO_{10}$, respectively. Milbemycin oxime is a macrocyclic lactone anthelmintic, containing two major factors, A_3 and A_4 of milbemycin oxime. The approximate ratio of A_3:A_4 is 20:80. Milbemycin A_4 5-oxime has the chemical composition of $C_{32}H_{45}NO_7$ and milbemycin A_3 5-oxime has the chemical composition of C31H43NO7.

Indications: COMBOGUARD is indicated for the prevention of heartworm disease (*Dirofilaria immitis*). COMBOGUARD kills fleas and is indicated for the prevention and treatment of flea infestations (*Ctenocephalides felis*), and the treatment and control of adult hookworm (*Ancylostoma caninum*), adult roundworm (*Toxocara canis* and *Toxascaris leonina*) and adult whipworm (*Trichuris vulpis*) infections in dogs and puppies 8 weeks of age or older and 5 pounds of body weight or greater.

Dosage and Administration: COMBOGUARD is given orally, once a month at the minimum dosage of 13.5 mg/lb (30 mg/kg) spinosad and 0.2 mg/lb (0.5 mg/kg) milbemycin oxime body weight. For heartworm prevention, give once monthly for at least 3 months after exposure to mosquitoes (see **EFFECTIVENESS**).

Dosage Schedule:

Body Weight	Spinosad Per Tablet (mg)	Milbemycin oxime Per Tablet (mg)	Tablets Administered
5 to 10 lbs	140	2.3	One
10.1 to 20 lbs	270	4.5	One
20.1 to 40 lbs	560	9.3	One
40.1 to 60 lbs	810	13.5	One
60.1 to 120 lbs	1620	27	One
Over 120 lbs	Administer the appropriate combination of tablets		

Administer COMBOGUARD with food for maximum effectiveness. To ensure heartworm prevention, owners should observe the dog for one hour after dosing. If vomiting occurs within an hour of administration, redose with another full dose. If a dose is missed and a monthly interval between doses is exceeded, then immediate administration of COMBOGUARD with food and resumption of monthly dosing will minimize the opportunity for the development of adult heartworm infections and flea reinfestations.

Heartworm Prevention:
COMBOGUARD should be administered at monthly intervals beginning within 1 month of the dog's first seasonal exposure and continuing until at least 3 months after the dog's last seasonal exposure to mosquitoes (see **EFFECTIVENESS**). COMBOGUARD may be administered year round without interruption. When replacing another heartworm preventative product, the first dose of COMBOGUARD should be given within a month of the last dose of the former medication.

Flea Treatment and Prevention:
Treatment with COMBOGUARD may begin at any time of the year, preferably starting one month before fleas become active and continuing monthly through the end of flea season. In areas where fleas are common year-round, monthly treatment with COMBOGUARD should continue the entire year without interruption.To minimize the likelihood of flea reinfestation, it is important to treat all animals within a household with an approved flea protection product.

Intestinal Nematode Treatment and Control:
COMBOGUARD also provides treatment and control of roundworms (*T. canis, T. leonina*), hookworms (*A. caninum*) and whipworms (*T. vulpis*). Dogs may be exposed to and can become infected with roundworms, whipworms and hookworms throughout the year, regardless of season or climate. Clients should be advised of measures to be taken to prevent reinfection with intestinal parasites.

Contraindications: There are no known contraindications to the use of COMBOGUARD.

Warnings: Not for human use. Keep this and all drugs out of the reach of children. Serious adverse reactions have been reported following concomitant extra-label use of ivermectin with spinosad alone, a component of COMBOGUARD (see **ADVERSE REACTIONS**).

Precautions: Treatment with fewer than 3 monthly doses after the last exposure to mosquitoes may not provide complete heartworm prevention (see **EFFECTIVENESS**).

Prior to administration of COMBOGUARD, dogs should be tested for existing heartworm infection. At the discretion of the veterinarian, infected dogs should be treated with an adulticide to remove adult heartworms. COMBOGUARD is not effective against adult *D. immitis*. While the number of circulating microfilariae may decrease following treatment, COMBOGUARD is not indicated for microfilariae clearance (see **ANIMAL SAFETY**).

Mild, transient hypersensitivity reactions manifested as labored respiration, vomiting, salivation and lethargy have been noted in some dogs treated with milbemycin oxime carrying a high number of circulating microfilariae. These reactions are presumably caused by release of protein from dead or dying microfilariae.

Use with caution in breeding females (see **ANIMAL SAFETY**). The safe use of COMBOGUARD in breeding males has not been evaluated.

Use with caution in dogs with pre-existing epilepsy (see **ADVERSE REACTIONS**).

Puppies less than 14 weeks of age may experience a higher rate of vomiting (see **ANIMAL SAFETY**).

Adverse Reactions: In a well-controlled US field study, which included a total of 352 dogs (176 treated with COMBOGUARD and 176 treated with an active control), no serious adverse reactions were attributed to administration of COMBOGUARD. All reactions were regarded as mild.

Over the 180-day study period, all observations of potential adverse reactions were recorded. Reactions that occurred at an incidence >1% (average monthly rate) within any of the 6 months of observation are presented in the following table. The most frequently reported adverse reaction in dogs in the COMBOGUARD group was vomiting.

Average Monthly Rate (%) of Dogs With Adverse Reactions

Adverse Reaction	COMBOGUARD Chewable Tablets[a]	Active Control Tablets[a]
Vomiting	6.13	3.08
Pruritus	4.00	4.91
Lethargy	2.63	1.54
Diarrhea	2.25	1.54
Dermatitis	1.47	1.45
Skin Reddening	1.37	1.26
Decreased appetite	1.27	1.35
Pinnal Reddening	1.18	0.87

[a]n=176 dogs

In the US field study, one dog administered COMBOGUARD experienced a single mild seizure 2 ½ hours after receiving the second monthly dose. The dog remained enrolled and received four additional monthly doses after the event and completed the study without further incident.

Following concomitant extra-label use of ivermectin with spinosad alone, a component of COMBOGUARD, some dogs have experienced the following clinical signs: *trembling/twitching, salivation/drooling, seizures, ataxia, mydriasis, blindness and disorientation*. Spinosad alone has been shown to be safe when administered concurrently with heartworm preventatives at label directions.

In US and European field studies, no dogs experienced seizures when dosed with spinosad alone at the therapeutic dose range of 13.5-27.3 mg/lb (30-60 mg/kg), including 4 dogs with pre-existing epilepsy. Four epileptic dogs that received higher than the maximum recommended dose of 27.3 mg/lb (60 mg/kg) experienced at least one seizure within the week following the second dose of spinosad, but no seizures following the first and third doses. The cause of the seizures observed in the field studies could not be determined.

For technical assistance or to report suspected adverse drug events, call 1-888-545-5973. For additional information about adverse drug experience reporting for animal drugs, contact FDA at 1-888-FDA-VETS or http://www.fda.gov/AnimalVeterinary/SafetyHealth

Post-Approval Experience (Mar 2012): The following adverse reactions are based on post-approval adverse drug event reporting. The adverse reactions are listed in decreasing order of frequency: vomiting, depression/lethargy, pruritus, anorexia, diarrhea, trembling/shaking, ataxia, seizures, hypersalivation and skin reddening.

Mode of Action: The primary target of action of spinosad, a component of COMBOGUARD, is an activation of nicotinic acetylcholine receptors (nAChRs) in insects. Spinosad does not interact with known insecticidal binding sites of other nicotinic or GABAergic insecticides such as neonicotinolds, fiproles, milbemycins, avermectins and cyclodienes. Insects treated with spinosad show involuntary muscle contractions and tremors resulting from activation of motor neurons. Prolonged spinosad-induced hyperexcitation results in prostration, paralysis and flea death. The selective toxicity of spinosad between insects and vertebrates may be conferred by the differential sensitivity of the insect versus vertebrate nAChRs.

Milbemycin oxime, a component of COMBOGUARD, acts by binding to glutamate-gated chloride ion channels in invertebrate nerve and muscle cells. Increased permeability by the cell membrane to chloride ions causes hyperpolarization of affected cells and subsequent paralysis and death of the intended parasites. Milbemycin oxime may also act by disrupting the transmission of invertebrate neurotransmitters, notably gamma amino butyric acid (GABA).

Effectiveness: *Heartworm Prevention:* In a well-controlled laboratory study, COMBOGUARD was 100% effective against induced heartworm infections when administered for 3 consecutive monthly doses. Two consecutive monthly doses did not provide 100% effectiveness against heartworm infection. In another well-controlled laboratory study, a single dose of COMBOGUARD was 100% effective against induced heartworm infections.

In a well-controlled six-month US field study conducted with COMBOGUARD, no dogs were positive for heartworm infection as determined by heartworm antigen testing performed at the end of the study and again three months later.

Flea Treatment and Prevention: In a well-controlled laboratory study, COMBOGUARD demonstrated 100% effectiveness on the first day following treatment and 100% effectiveness on Day 30. In a well-controlled laboratory study, spinosad, a component of COMBOGUARD, began to kill fleas 30 minutes after administration and demonstrated 100% effectiveness within 4 hours. Spinosad, a component of COMBOGUARD, kills fleas before they can lay eggs. If a severe environmental infestation exists, fleas may persist for a period of time after dose administration due to the emergence of adult fleas from pupae already in the environment. In field studies conducted in households with existing flea infestations of varying severity, flea reductions of 98.0% to 99.8% were observed over the course of 3 monthly treatments with spinosad alone. Dogs with signs of flea allergy dermatitis showed improvement in erythema, papules, scaling, alopecia, dermatitis/pyodermatitis and pruritus as a direct result of eliminating the fleas.

Treatment and Control of Intestinal Nematode Infections: In well-controlled laboratory studies, COMBOGUARD was ≥ 90% effective in removing naturally and experimentally induced adult roundworm, whipworm and hookworm infections.

Palatability: COMBOGUARD is a flavored chewable tablet. In a field study of client-owned dogs where 175 dogs were each offered COMBOGUARD once a month for 6 months, dogs voluntarily consumed 54% of the doses when offered plain as if a treat, and 33% of the doses when offered in or on food. The remaining 13% of doses were administered like other tablet medications.

Animal Safety: COMBOGUARD was tested in pure and mixed breeds of healthy dogs in well-controlled clinical and laboratory studies. No dogs were withdrawn from the field studies due to treatment-related adverse reactions.

In a margin of safety study, COMBOGUARD was administered orally to 8-week-old Beagle puppies at doses of 1, 3 and 5 times the upper half of the therapeutic dose band, every 28 days for 6 dosing periods. Vomiting was seen in all groups including control animals with similar frequency. Adverse reactions seen during the course of the study were salivation, tremors, decreased activity, coughing and vocalization.

Body weights were similar between control and treated groups throughout the study. Treatment with COMBOGUARD was not associated with any clinically significant hematology, clinical chemistry or gross necropsy changes. One 5X dog had minimal glomerular lipidosis observed microscopically. The clinical relevance of this finding is unknown.

Plasma spinosyn A, spinosyn D, milbemycin A3 5-oxime and milbemycin A4 5-oxime concentrations increased throughout the study. At each dosing period, plasma spinosyn A and spinosyn D concentrations were greater than proportional across the dose range 1 to 5X. Plasma milbemycin A4 5-oxime concentrations appeared to be dose proportional across range 1 to 5X by the end of the study. Plasma concentrations of spinosad and milbemycin oxime indicate that expected systemic exposures were achieved throughout the study.

In an avermectin-sensitive Collie dog study, COMBOGUARD was administered orally at 1, 3 and 5 times the upper half of the recommended therapeutic dose band every 28 days. No signs of avermectin sensitivity were observed after administration of COMBOGUARD during the study period to avermectin-sensitive Collie dogs. The adverse reactions observed in the treatment groups were vomiting and diarrhea. Body weights in all treatment groups were comparable to the control group. Hematology and clinical chemistry parameters showed no clinically significant changes from study start to end, and all dogs were considered healthy throughout the study.

In a heartworm-positive safety study, COMBOGUARD was administered orally at 1, 3 and 5 times the upper half of the therapeutic dose band to Beagle dogs with adult heartworm infections and circulating microfilariae, every 28 days for 3 treatments. Vomiting was observed in one dog in the 1X group, in three dogs in the 3X group and in one dog in the 5X group. All but one incident of vomiting was observed on the treatment day during the first treatment cycle. The vomiting was mild and self-limiting. Hypersensitivity reactions were not observed in any of the treatment groups. Microfilariae counts decreased with treatment.

In a reproductive safety study, COMBOGUARD was administered orally to female dogs at 1 and 3 times the upper half of the therapeutic dose band every 28 days prior to mating, during gestation and during a six-week lactation period. Dogs with confirmed fetal heartbeats on ultrasound examination were evaluated for reproductive safety. One 3X and one 1X group female did not become pregnant. No treatment-related adverse reactions or signs of avermectin toxicosis were noted for adult females. Adult females in the 3X group lost weight during the 6-week pre-mating period, while control group females gained weight during that time. The body weights of the treated groups were comparable to the control group during gestation and post-parturition phases of the study. Gestation length, litter average body weight, litter size, stillborn pups, pup survival and the proportion of pups with malformations were comparable between treated and control dam groups. Malformations in the 1X group included a pup with cleft palate and a littermate with anophthalmia, fused single nares, misshapen palate, hydrocephalus, omphalocele and malpositioned testes; a pup with a malformation of the anterior tip of the urinary bladder and umbilical blood vessel; and a pup with patent ductus arteriosus (PDA). Malformations in the 3X group included three littermates with PDA. Malformations in the control group included a pup with a malformed sternum and a pup with PDA and a malpositioned superior vena cava. Clinical findings in pups of the treated groups were comparable to the control group except for one 1X group pup that was smaller and less coordinated than its littermates and had tremors when excited. The relationship between spinosad and milbemycin oxime treatment and the 1X and 3X dogs that did not become pregnant, the specific pup malformations and the unthrifty 1X group pup are unknown. The incidence of cleft palate is not unexpected based on the historical data collected at the breeding site.

In a margin of safety study with spinosad alone, 6-week old Beagle puppies were administered average doses of 1.5, 4.4 and 7.4 times the maximum recommended dose at 28-day intervals over a 6-month period. Vomiting was observed across all treatments, including controls, and was observed at an increased rate at elevated doses. Vomiting most often occurred 1 hour following administration and decreased over time and stabilized when puppies reached 14 weeks of age.

Storage Information: Store at 20-25°C (68-77°F), excursions permitted between 15-30°C (59-86°F).

How Supplied: COMBOGUARD is available in five tablet sizes. Each tablet size is available in color-coded packages of 6 tablets.

5-10 lbs (140 mg spinosad and 2.3 mg milbemycin oxime)
10.1-20 lbs (270 mg spinosad and 4.5 mg milbemycin oxime)
20.1-40 lbs (560 mg spinosad and 9.3 mg milbemycin oxime)
40.1-60 lbs (810 mg spinosad and 13.5 mg milbemycin oxime)
60.1-120 lbs (1620 mg spinosad and 27 mg milbemycin oxime)

NADA 141-321, Approved by the FDA

Distributed by Vicar Operating, Inc.
12401 West Olympic Blvd. Los Angeles, CA 90064

www.vethical.com

All trademarks are the property of their respective owners. All rights reserved.

NDC 50386-4332-7   CA4332Y07AMC1   NDC 50386-4333-7   CA4333Y07AMC1
NDC 50386-4334-7   CA4334Y07AMC1   NDC 50386-4335-7   CA4335Y07AMC1
NDC 50386-4336-7   CA4336Y07AMC1

03B081   Dec 2014   Mkt1